Max
And his Big Imagination

 **DINOSAUR ACTIVITY BOOK**

by
Chrissy Metge

© Chrissy Metge 2019

www.chrissymetge.com
www.ducklingpublishing.com

USBN: 978-0-473-44103-6

all about me

All about:

This is me:

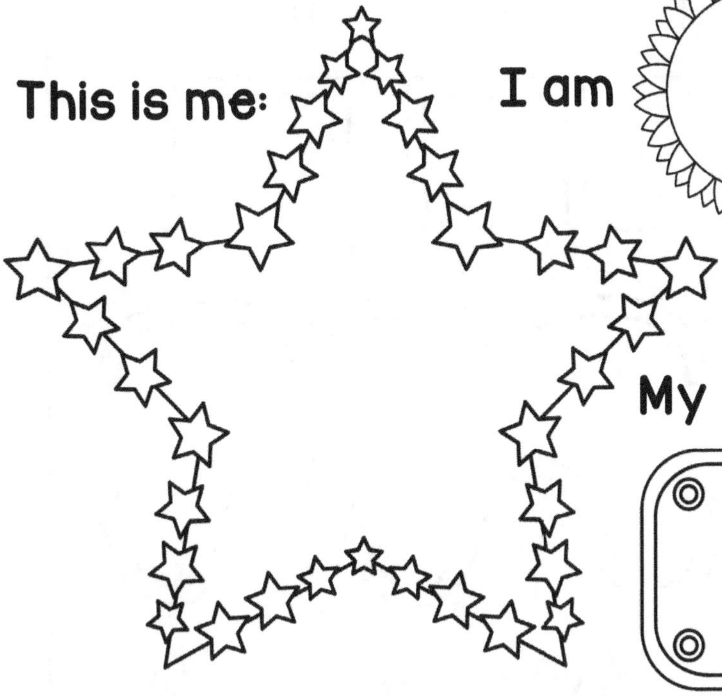

I am  [ ] years old.

My favorite colour:

My birthday:

 WARM UP WORK

Follow the lines.

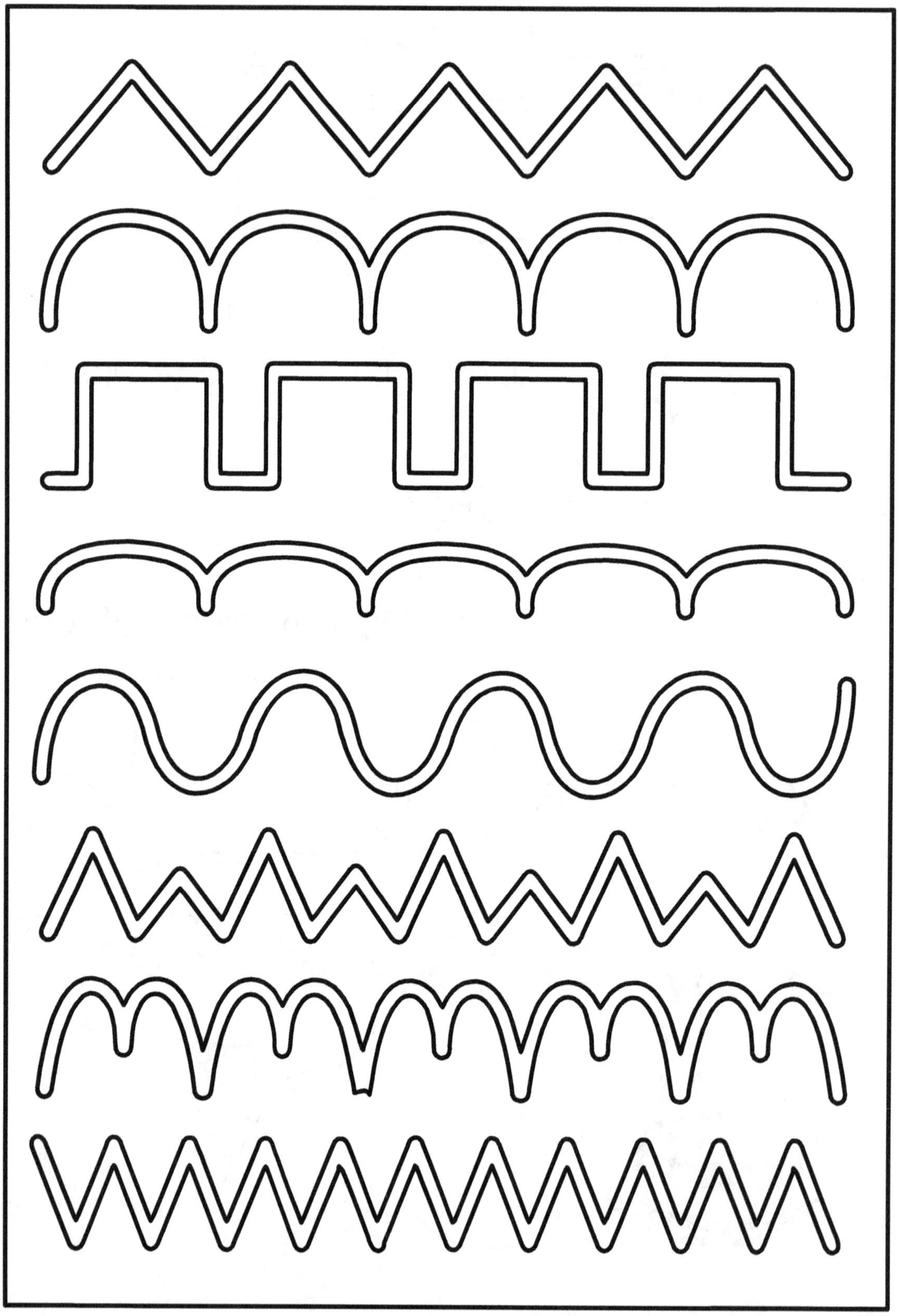

 DRAW IN THE SHAPES

Fill in the shapes with anything you want!

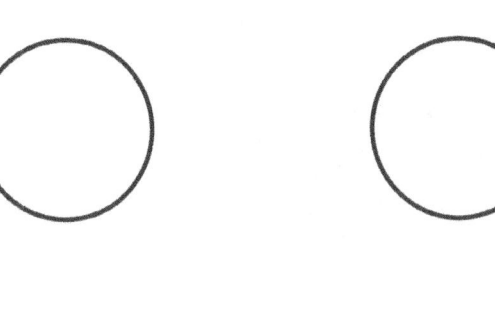

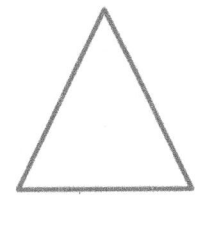
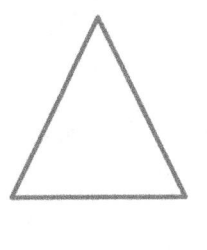

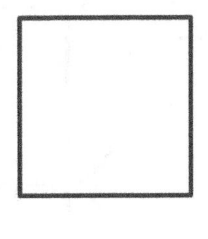

 DRAW IN THE SHAPES

Fill in the shapes with anything you want!

 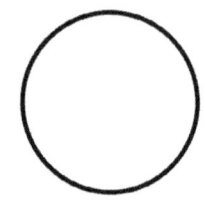 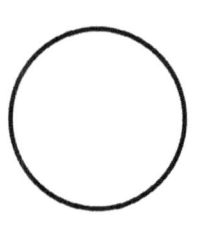

 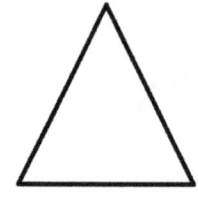 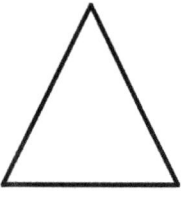

 COLOUR THE DINOSAUR

Use the colour key to colour the dinosaur.

1 = blue   3 = brown   5 = green
2 = pink   4 = yellow   6 = orange

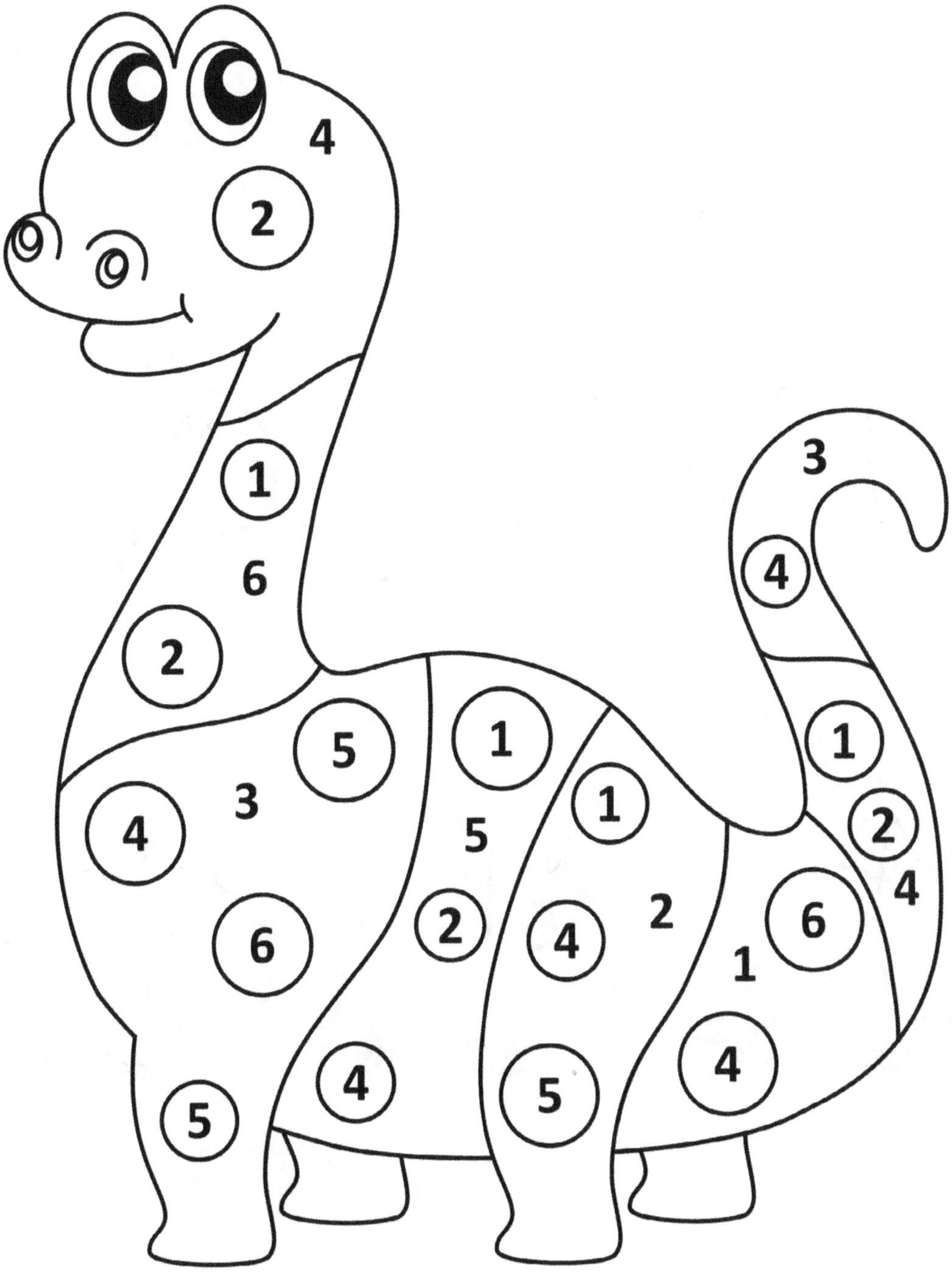

HOW TO DRAW

Learn how to draw a dinosaur!

HOW TO DRAW

Draw your dinosaur here.

FIND THE PATH

Help the dinosaur find more trees to eat!

 DRAW A PICTURE

Draw your own dinosaur hatching out of this egg.

 # FINISH THE DRAWING

Finish the rest of this dinosaur.

 CONNECT THE DOTS

Connect the numbered dots to finish the picture.

FIND THE NUMBERS

Write the missing numbers.

1 2 3 4 5
6 7 8 9 10
11 12 13 14 15
16 17 18
19 20

 CONNECT THE DOTS

Connect the numbered dots to finish the picture.

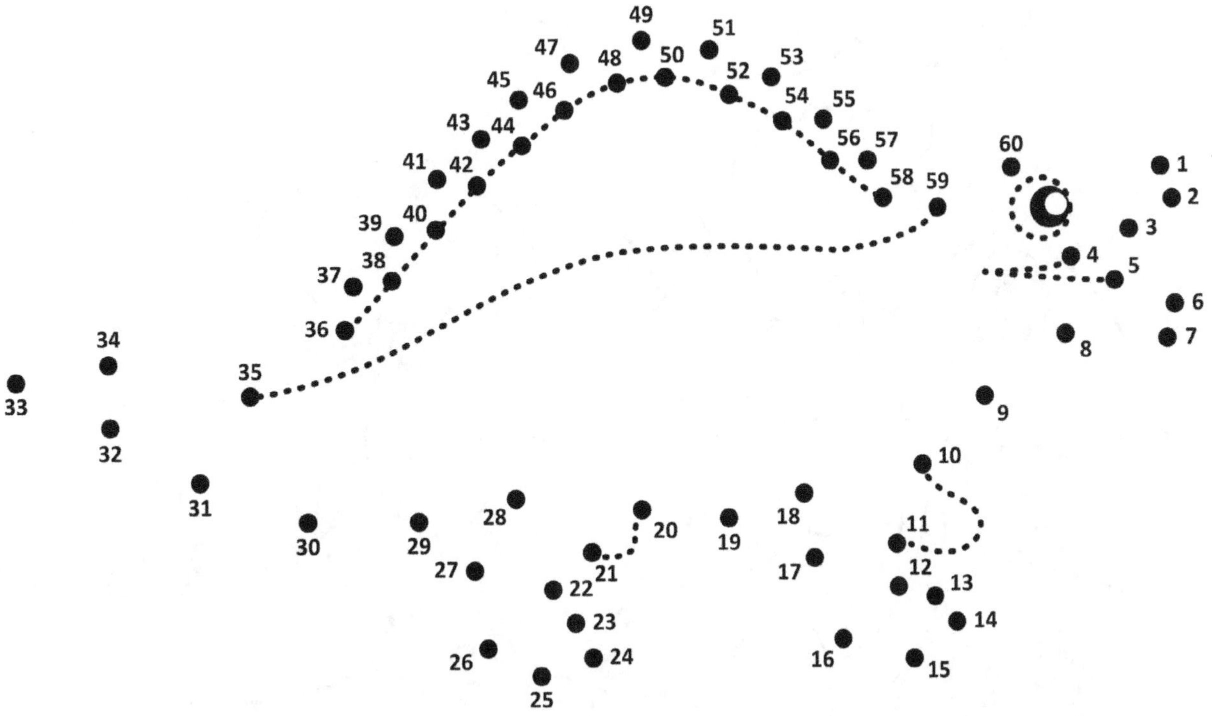

COLOUR A PICTURE

Colour the dinosaur.

FIND THE PATHS

Find the paths through the maze.

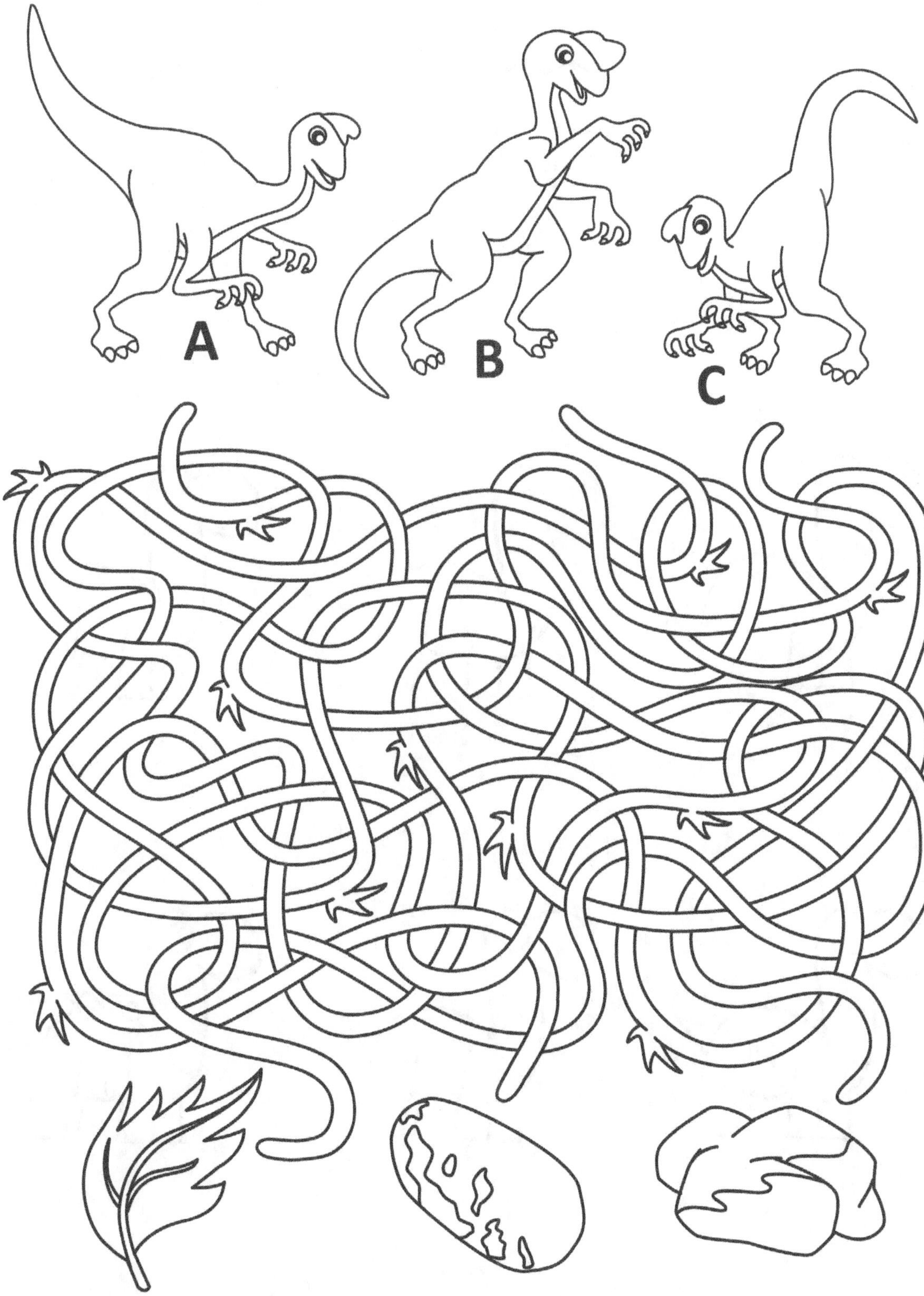

HOW TO DRAW

Learn how to draw a dinosaur!

HOW TO DRAW

Draw your dinosaur here.

LETTER MAZE

Help T-Rex find her mother! Draw a line from letter to letter in alphabetical order.

FINISH THE DRAWING

Draw the dinosaurs tail.

 COLOUR A PICTURE

Colour the dinosaur!

 NUMBER TRACE

Trace the numbers from 1 to 10.

HOW TO DRAW

Learn how to draw a dinosaur!

HOW TO DRAW

Draw your dinosaur here.

MATCH THE LETTERS

Match the capital letter to the correct lowercase letter on the dinosaur eggs!

A	 🦖	r a t
B	 🦕	f j b
C	 🦕	c w k
D	 🦕	d g p
E	 🦅	s e m

DESIGN YOUR OWN DINOSAURS

Finish the pictures!

FIND AND COUNT

Count and colour the dinosaurs. Record the number.

 MATCH THE PICTURES

Draw a line to the right dinosaur shadow.

 D IS FOR DINOSAUR

Learn to write the letter D.

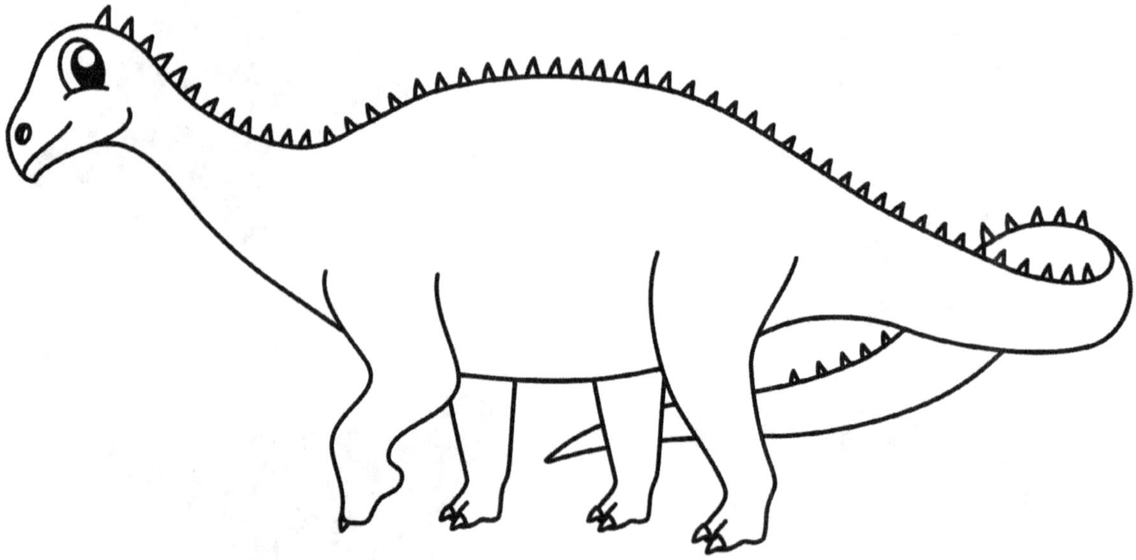

 TRACE AND COLOUR

Trace and design your own footprint and cut it out.

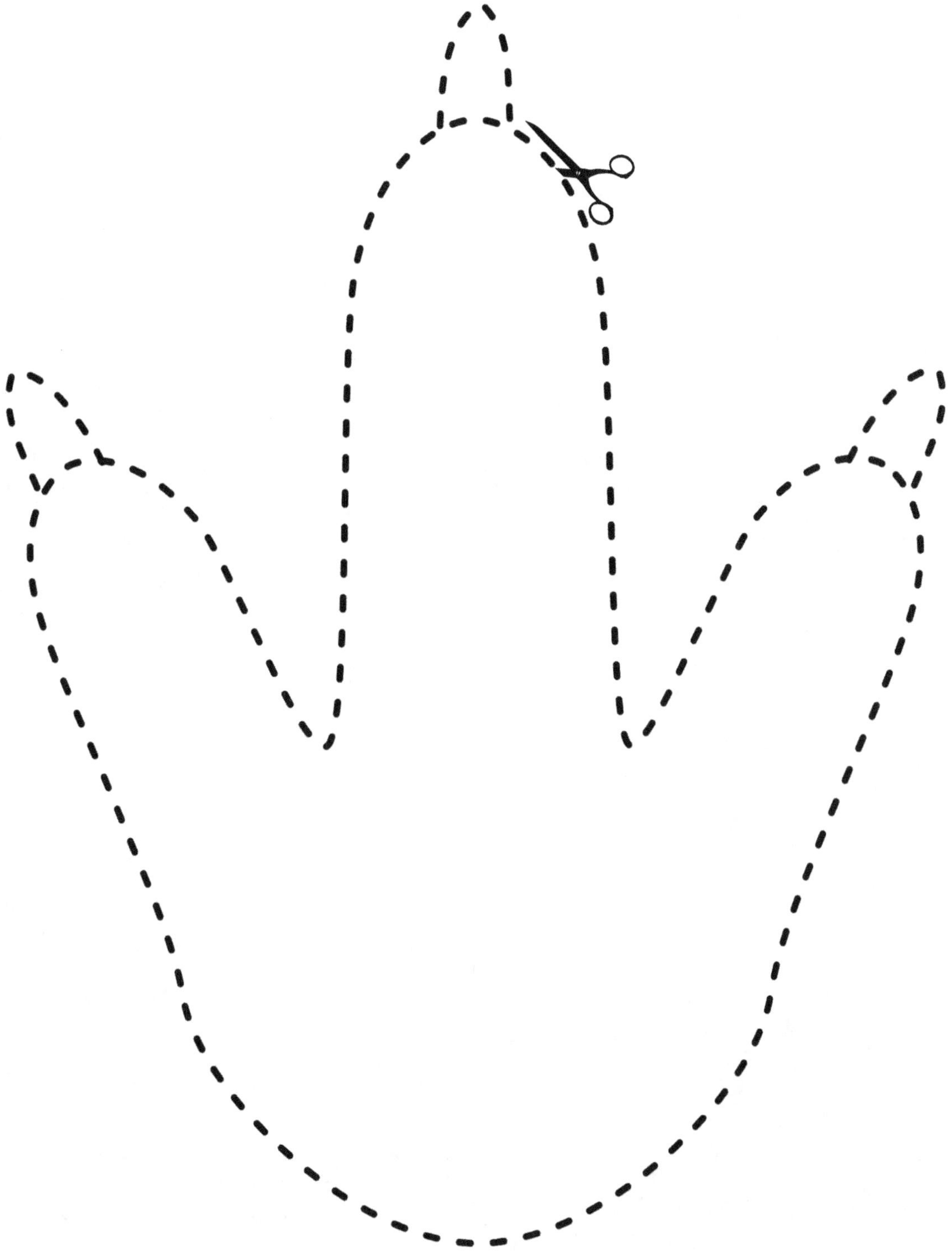

 COLOUR AND CUT

Colour and cut out your own dinosaur mask!

 WHAT COMES NEXT?

Cut out and find the matching picture.

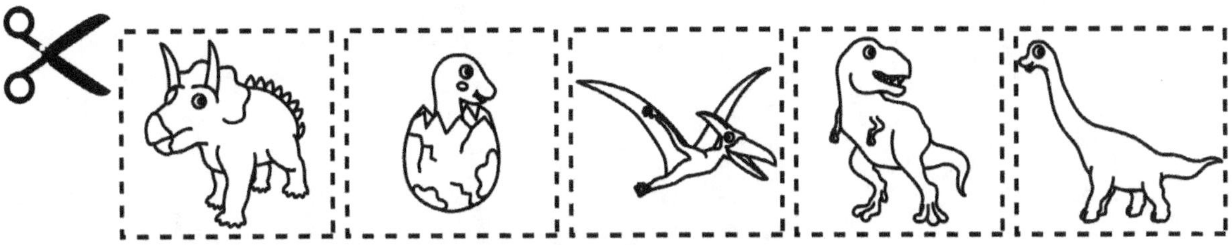

 # COLOUR AND CUT

Cut out and match the dinosaurs up.

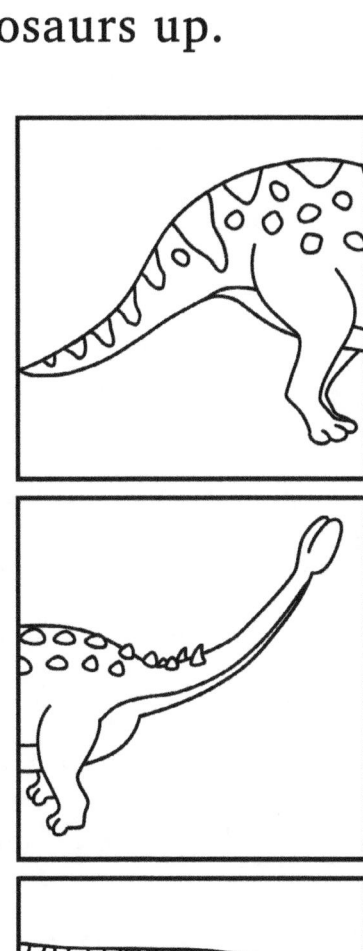

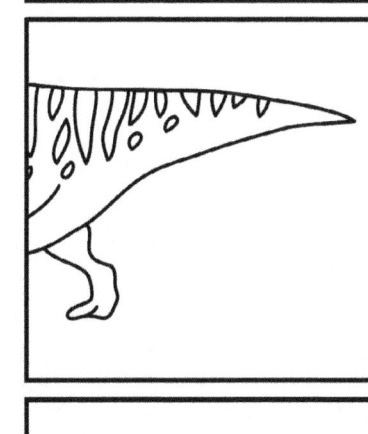

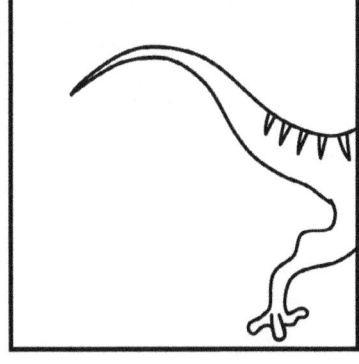

37

Max and his Big Imagination: Dinosaur Activity Book

CUT AND LABEL

Cut out the labels below.
Glue them onto the correct part of the dinsosaur.

tail   nose

spikes   legs   teeth

Max And his Big Imagination

Check out our other activity books!

Transport Activity Book
Space Activity Book
Dinosaur Activity Book
Seaside Activity Book

Read, Play, Imagine!

www.ducklingpublishing.com

www.ingramcontent.com/pod-product-compliance
Lightning Source LLC
Chambersburg PA
CBHW081436300426
44108CB00016BA/2384